ISBN: 0-89898-180-8

© 1983 DOORS MUSIC CO.

THE
doors

Light My Fire

Words and Music by
THE DOORS

Copyright © 1967 Doors Music Co.
International Copyright Secured Made In U.S.A. All Rights Reserved

Am7
F♯m7
G
A
Girl, we could-n't get much higher;
love be-come a fune-ral pyre.
1. 2. Come on, ba-by, light my fire,
D
G
A
D
B
G
D
Come on, ba-by, light my fire,
Try to set the night on
E
1.
2
f
fire.
2. The
2. The
cresc.
Am7
F♯m7
Am7
time to hes-i-tate is through,
No time to wal-low in the mire,
f
F♯m7
Am7
F♯m7
Try now we can on-ly lose,
And our

Am7
F♯m7
G
A
love be-come a fune-ral pyre.
Come on, ba-by, light my fire,
D
G
A
D
Come on, ba-by, light my fire,
F
C
D
(repeat 3 times)
F
C
Try to set the night on fire,
Try to set the night on
ff
D
G
D
fire.
F
B♭
E♭
A♭
A♮

Hello, I Love You

(Won't You Tell Me Your Name?)

Words and Music by
THE DOORS

With a beat

Copyright © 1968 Doors Music Co.
International Copyright Secured Made In U.S.A. All Rights Reserved

A G A G A G A D
make the queen of the an-gels sigh? Hel- lo, I love you, Won't you tell me your name? Hel-
A G A D A G
lo, I love you let me jump in your game, Hel- lo, I love you, won't you
A D A G A D
tell me your name? Hel- lo, I love you, let me jump in your game. She
A G A G A G
holds her head so high like a stat - ue in the
A G A G A G
sky Her arms are wick-ed and her legs are long. When she

- Repeat and fade -

Been Down So Long

Lyrics by JIM MORRISON
Music by THE DOORS

Copyright © 1971 Doors Music Co.
International Copyright Secured Made In U.S.A. All Rights Reserved

Em
B
Bb
Now, why don't one of you peo - ple
A N.C.
Em
c' - mon and set me free?
Em
Em
I said, war - den, war - den, war - den,
Em
won't you break your lock and key.
Em
A7
I said, war - den, war - den,

A7
war - den,
won't you break
your lock and
Em
key.
Hey,
B
Bb
A
N.C.
come a - long here, mis - ter,
c'mon,
and let the poor boy
Em
be.
Em
Em
Ba - by, ba - by, ba - by,
won't you get

Em
down on your knee;
Em
A7
Ba - by, Ba - by,
A7
G
A7
Ba - by,
won't you get down on your
Em
knee.
Em
B
B♭
C' - mon, lit-tle dar - lin',

A
N.C.
Em
C'-mon
and give your love to
me.
Em
Well, I been
A
N.C.
A7
N.C.
A7
N.C.
A7
C'-mon,
c'-mon,
c'-mon,
loco
A7
N.C.
3
Em
E♭7
E7
and set me free!

You Make Me Real

Words and Music by
JIM MORRISON

Copyright © 1970 Doors Music Co.
International Copyright Secured Made In U.S.A. All Rights Reserved

You make me
real, __
you make me
on - ly
F7
C7
feel
you
like lov-ers feel. __
have that ap - peal. __
You make me
So let me
G
F
N.C.
C
N.C.
throw a-way mis-tak - en mis - er - y. __
slide in your ten - der sunk - en sea, _
Make me
free, love. Make me
free, love, Make me
C
free.
C
N.C.
C
N.C.
free,
Make me
free.
You
make me
(Drums)
C7(♭5)
real. __

Wild Child

Words and Music by
THE DOORS

Copyright © 1969 Doors Music Co.
International Copyright Secured Made In U.S.A. All Rights Reserved

Gm Bb Gm
Gm Bb Gm
Gm Bb Gm
Na-tu-ral child,
ter-ri-ble child.
Not your moth-er's or your
Gm Gm
Gm Bb Gm
Gm Bb Gm
fath-er's child. You're
our child
scream-in' wild.
A
Ab
N.C.
Drums
G F G
G F G
Bb B
With
hun-ger at her heels
C Cb
Bb B
C Cb
free-dom in her eyes, she
dan-ces on her knees,
pi-rate prince at her

Bb
A
Ab
G
side.
Drums
Star-ing
in-to
the hol-low id-ol's eye
G
C
Dm
Wild child
C
G
C
full of grace
sav-ior of the
hu - man race
8va basso
G7
C
G7
your cool face
your cool face
8va
C
G9
C
G
your cool face
8va
(spoken)
"You remember when we were in Africa"

Tell All The People

Words and Music by
ROBBIE KRIEGER

Copyright © 1969 Doors Music Co.
International Copyright Secured Made In U.S.A. All Rights Reserved

E
F#7
Tell all the peo-ple that you see set them
Can't you see me grow-ing, get your guns the time has
A
A E B7 E
free fol-low me down.
come to fol-low me down.
G
E
You tell them they don't have to run
G
E
we're gon-na pick up ever-y-one
G
D
come on, take me by the hand gon-na

C
G6 D7 G
bu - ry all our trou-bles in the sand. Oh
B
F♯mi
B
yeah!
R.H.
E
Fol - low me a - cross the sea where milk - y ba - bies seem to be
A
F♯
mold - ed flow - ing re - vel - ry with the one that set them free
E
F♯7
Tell All The Peo - ple that you see it's

A
A E B13 E
just me
fol - low me down
B
F#m7
B
E
F#7
Tell All The Peo - ple that you see
fol - low
A
A E B7 E
me
fol - low me down.
E
F#7
Tell All The Peo-ple that you see
we'll be
fol - low

A
A E B7 E
free
me
fol-low me down.
E
F♯7
Fol-low me down, you got to fol-low me down,
A
A E A6 E
fol-low me down
E
F♯7
Tell All The Peo-ple that you see we'll be
A
A E A6 E
free
fol-low me down
(repeat and fade)

The Soft Parade

"When I was back there in seminary school,
there was a person there who put forth the
proposition that you can petition the Lord
with prayer ...
petition the Lord with prayer...petition
the Lord with prayer...petition the Lord
with prayer.
You cannot petition the Lord with prayer!"

Words and Music by
JIM MORRISON

Copyright © 1969 Doors Music Co.
International Copyright Secured Made In U.S.A. All Rights Reserved

Am Dm7 E 13 Am
soft a - sy - lum? I can't make it an-y-more; The man is at the door.
Fast (in 2)
Gm7 Abm7 Am7 Bbm7 Am7 Abm7 Gm7 Abm7 Am7
Bbm7 Am7 Eb9 Abmaj7 Ab
Gm7 Abm7 Am7 Bbm7 Am7 Abm7 Gm Abm7 Am7
Pep - per - mint mi - ni - skirts, cho - co - late
Cham - pi - on sax and a girl named
Bbm7 Am7(b5) Ab7 Gm Abm7 Am7 Bbm7 Am7 Eb7
can - dy,
San - dy;

1.
Abmaj7
2.
Abmaj7
Guitar Solo
Bbm7
Eb7
Ab
Abmaj7
Gb
Eb
Abm7
There's
Gm Abm7 Am7 Bbm7 Am7 Abm7 Gm Abm7 Am7
1.
Bbm7 Am7(b5) Ab7
on - ly four ways to get un - rav - eled;
one is to sleep and the oth - er is
2.
Bbm7 Eb7
Abmaj7
trav - el,

Gm Abm7 Am7 Bbm7 Am7 Abm7 Gm Abm7 Am7 Bbm7 Am7 Abm7
one is a band it up in the hills,
Gm Abm7 Am7 Bbm7 Am7 Abm7 Gm7 Abm7 Am7 Bb7
one is to love your neigh - bor till his
Twice as slowly (in 4)
C C Cmaj7 Dm C Em Dm C Em Dm
wife gets home.
C Cmaj7 Dm C Dm C Dm C Em Dm
Ca - ta-combs, nurse-ry bones, win - ter wo - men
C Dm C Dm C Dm C Dm
grow-ing stones, carry-ing ba-bies to the riv-er;

C
Dm
Streets and shoes,
av-en-ues,
leath-er rid-ers sell-ing news.
The
monk bought
lunch.
E
N.C.
Em
Bm
E7
Suc-cess-ful hills are here to stay.
A
Ever-y-thing must be this way.
Gen-tle street where peo-ple play,

A Em E7 A Em
wel-come to the soft par-ade. All our lives we sweat and save,
B7 Em E7 A Em
build-ing for a shal - low grave. "Must be some-thing else" we say,
B7 Em E7 A Em
"some-how to de-fend this place." Ever-y-thing must be this way,
B7 Em Em Bm Em Bm
ever-y-thing must be this way.
Em E7 A Em
The soft par-ade has now be-gun; lis-ten to the en- gines hum.

E7
A
B7
N.C.
Peo-ple out to have_ some fun,
co-bra on my left,
leop-ard on my
Em
right.
Deer wo-man in a
silk dress,
A
Em
E7
girls with beads a-round their necks,
kiss the hun-ter of the
green vest who has
A
B♭
B
N.C.
Em
wrest-led be-fore
with li-ons_ in the
night.
E
Out of sight!_
The
lights are get-ting bright - er,

The ra- di- o is moan - ing,
call-in' to the dogs there are still a few an - i-mals
left out in the yard, but it's get-ting hard - er
to de - scribe sail - ors to the
un-der - fed

(Spoken:)
Trop-ic cor-ri-dor, trop-ic treas-ure. What got us this far, to this mild E-qua-tor?
We need someone or some-thing new, some-thin' else to get us through.
1st voice
2nd voice
(Left hand continues same pattern till the end.)
But it's get-ting
Call-in' on the dogs, call-in' on the dogs, call-in' on the dogs
hard - er,
call-in' on the dogs.
call-in' on the dogs, call-in' on the dogs.
You got-ta
3rd voice
8va
shoot at a few an - i-mals left out in the yard
meet me at the cross - roads.
Too late, ba-by! Too late!

8va

1st voice: but it's get-tin' much hard-er.

8va

2nd voice: Got-ta meet me at the edge of town,

3rd voice: (Half-spoken:) Trop-ic cor-ri-dor,

8va

1st voice: You'd bet-ter come a-long. Just you and I

8va

2nd voice: out-skirts of the cit-y. We were so a - lone.

3rd voice: trop-ic treas-ure.

8va

Fade out

1st voice: Bet-ter bring your gun. You'd bet-ter bring your gun. (spoken passage)*

8va

2nd voice: Bet-ter bring your gun

3rd voice: (Half-spoken:) Trop-ic cor-ri-dor, trop-ic treas-ure.

4

*(Spoken ad lib over instrumental)

When all else fails, we can whip the horses' eyes and make them sleep and cry.

Riders On The Storm

Words and Music by
THE DOORS

Copyright © 1971 Doors Music Co.
International Copyright Secured Made In U.S.A. All Rights Reserved

Em A Am Bm/A C/A D/A
In - to this house we're born, in -

Em A Em A D
to this world we're thrown like a dog with - out a bone, an

C Em A Em7 A
act - or out on loan. Ri - ders on the storm. There's a

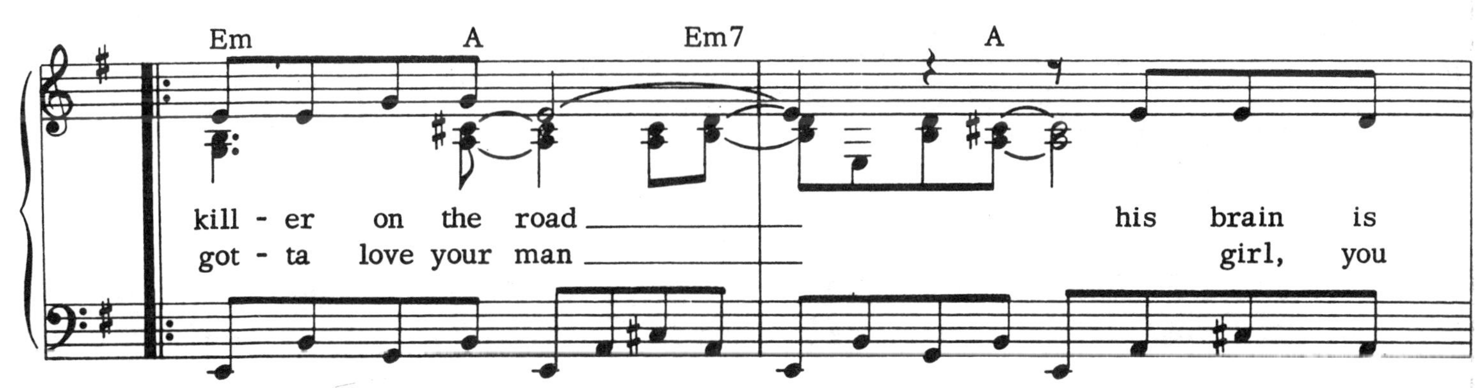
Em A Em7 A
kill - er on the road his brain is
got - ta love your man girl, you

Em
A
Em7
A
Am
Bm/A
squirm-ing like a toad.
Take a long hol - i day
got - ta love your man.
Take him by the hand

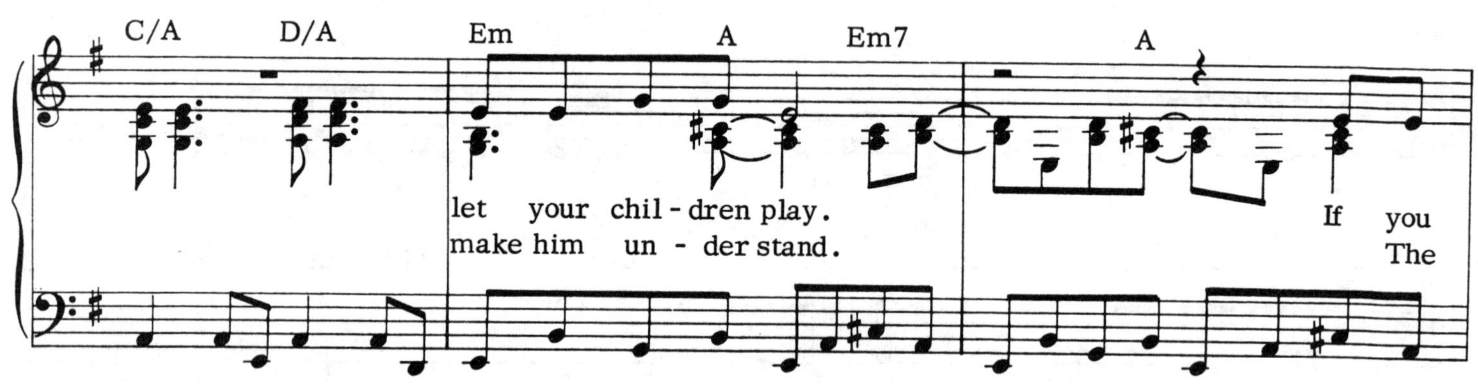
C/A
D/A
Em
A
Em7
A
let your chil-dren play.
If you
make him un - der stand.
The

D
C
Em
A
give this man a ride, sweet
fam-i - ly will die.
Kill-er on the road.
world on you de-pends, our
life will nev-er end. You
got-ta love your man.

A
Em
A
Em7
A
1.
Em
Em7

A
2.
Em
A
Em7
A
2. Girl, you
Em7
A
Em
A
Em7
A
Em
A
Em7
Em7
A
Em9
A
Em9
Riders on the storm,
A
Em9
Riders on the storm,
Em9
A
Em9
Riders on the storm,
A
Em9
Riders on the storm,
Em9
Repeat and fade

My Eyes Have Seen You

Words and Music by
THE DOORS

Copyright © 1967 Doors Music Co.
International Copyright Secured Made In U.S.A. All Rights Reserved

G
Em D Em
Em D Em
meet in-side
fix your hair
show me some more
move up stairs,
show me some more
move up stairs
1.
Em D Em
show me some more. My
2.
Em D Em
move up-stairs. My
Em D Em
eyes have seen you,
B7 Em
My
Em D Em
eyes have seen you,
B7 Em
My
E
eyes have seen you
D
free from dis - guise,
G
gaz-ing on a ci - ty un - der
Em D Em
tel - e - vi - sion skies,
Em Dm Em
tel - e - vi-sion skies,
Em D Em
tel - e - vi-sion skies.

Em D EmD Em D Em D Em Em D Em Dm Em
D Em D Em Em
My eyes have seen you,
D Em D Em
Em
eyes have seen you,
D Em D Em
E
eyes have seen you let them
D
pho - to - graph your soul,
G
mem-o-rize your al-leys on an
Em D Em D Em D Em D Em
end-less roll, end-less roll.
(repeat ad lib)

I Looked At You

Words and Music by
THE DOORS

I Looked At You - 3 - 1

Copyright © 1966 Doors Music Co.
International Copyright Secured Made In U.S.A. All Rights Reserved

C
No, we can't turn back, babe;
Yeah, we're on our way;
G7
And we can't turn back
C
'cause it's too
Cm
late, too
B♭
late, too
A♭
late, too
G♭
late, too
G7
late.
And we're on our way.
No, we can't turn back,

C
G7
babe;
Yeah, we're on our way;
And we can't turn back.
C
F7
C7
F
C
A♭
C
F
G
C
D. S.
late,
too
la - te.

Do It

Words and Music by
JIM MORRISON and
ROBBIE KRIEGER

Copyright © 1969 Doors Music Co.
International Copyright Secured Made In U.S.A. All Rights Reserved

G
G6
Please, please, lis-ten to me, chil-dren.
Please, please, lis-ten to me, chil-dren.
G6
C
D
G (N.C.)
You are the ones who will rule the world.
(Drums Solo)
A
You got-ta pleasc me
A7
D
A
A7
D
A
all night.
sfz
sfz

G
G6
Please, please, lis-ten to me, chil-dren
said
A
A6
please, please, lis-ten to me chil -dren.
G
8va
Em(9 add)
Please
Yeah,
please me.
(Drums)
(Drums)
8va
F♯m(G bass)
8va
8va
A
D

8va
B
N.C.
(Drums)
sfz
A
Please, please lis-ten to me chil-
A6
dren.
A
Please, my
A6
chil - dren.
A
Please,
A6
chil - dren.
A
Please,
N.C.
chil - dren.
f

Break On Through

3. I found an island in your arms, a country in your eyes,
Arms that chain, eyes that lie.... Break on Through, etc.

4. Made the scene from week to week, day to day, hour to hour,
The gate is straight, deep and wide....Break on Through, etc.

Copyright © 1966 Doors Music Co.
International Copyright Secured Made In U.S.A. All Rights Reserved

oth - er side,__ Break on thru__ to the oth - er side.__

Em (to end)

-(two times)-

-(four times)-

Ev - 'ry - bod - y loves my ba - by. She gets.

(8va to end)

-(four times)-

Break on thru,__ Break, Break. Break.

-(four times)- -(four times)-

Love Street

Copyright © 1968 Doors Music Co.
International Copyright Secured Made In U.S.A. All Rights Reserved

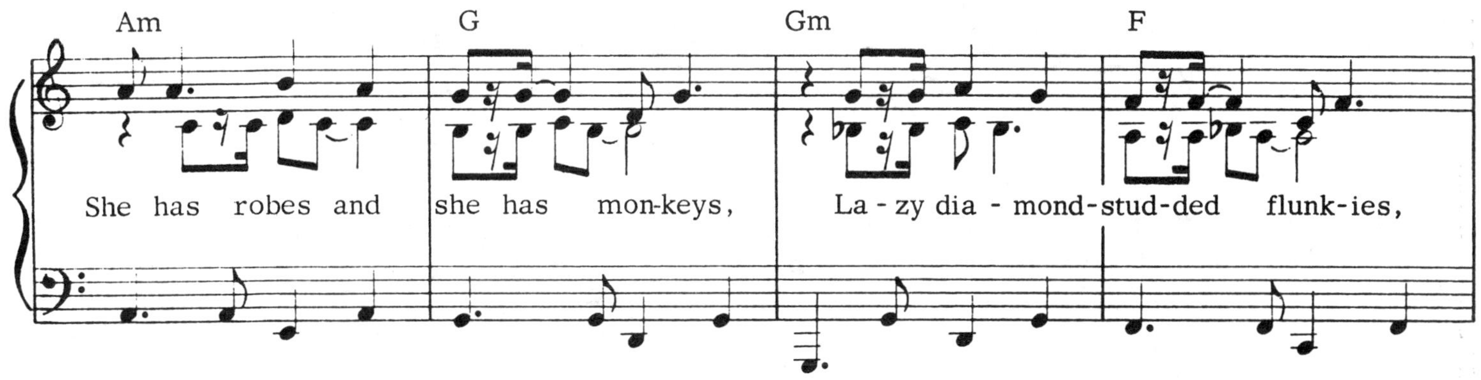
Am
G
Gm
F
She has robes and she has mon-keys, La - zy dia - mond - stud - ded flunk - ies,

Gm
Am
B♭
She has wis - dom and knows what to do,

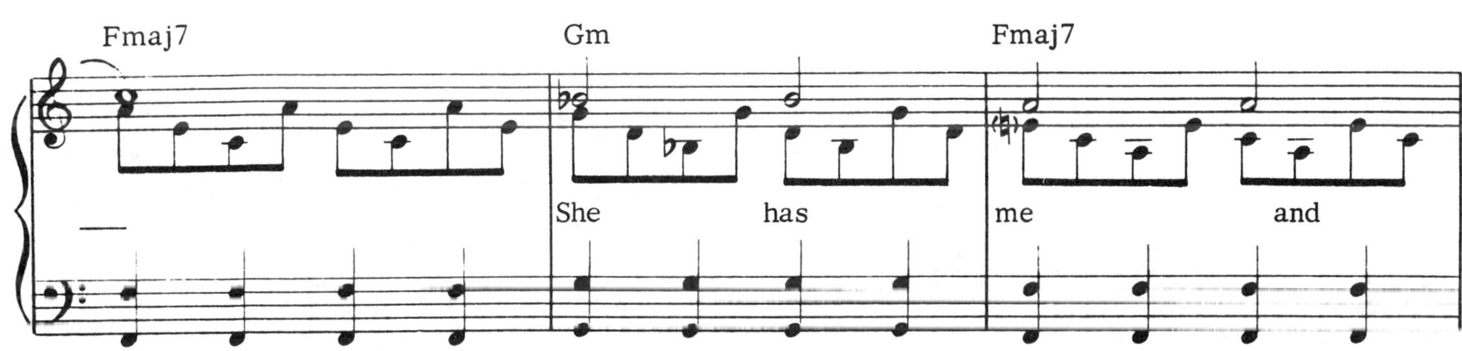
Fmaj7
Gm
Fmaj7
She has me and

B♭6
A7(4 sus)
A7
she has you.

Bm
A
Am
G
Bm
A
Am
G
Am
Bm
She has wis - dom and
C
Gmaj7
Am7
Gmaj7
knows what to do,
She has me and

C6
G
Am
she
has
you.
repeat 3 times
Spoken:
Am
G
Gm
F
1. I see you live on Love Street;
There's the store where the creatures meet.
2. I wonder what they do in there,
Summer Sunday and a year.
3. I guess I like it fine so far.
Gm
F
C
D
Bm
A
Am
G
She lives on Love Street, Lingers long on Love Street.
Bm
A
Am
G
She has a house and garden I would like to see what happens.
(repeat and fade)

Peace Frog

Lyrics by JIM MORRISON
Music by THE DOORS

Copyright © 1970 Doors Music Co.
International Copyright Secured Made In U.S.A. All Rights Reserved

Gm C7 Gm C7

Just a - bout the break of day.

Gm C7 Em

She came, then she drove_a-way,_

B7 A Gm C7

sun-light in her hair._ Blood on the streets runs a riv-er of sad - ness._

Gm C7 Gm C7

Blood in the streets, it's up to my thigh._

Gm C7 Gm C7

The riv-er runs down the legs of the cit - y;

Gm
C7
Gm
C7
The wom-en are cry-ing red riv-ers of weep - ing.
Gm
C7
Em
She came in town and then she went_ a-way,_
B7
A
Ab
sun-light in her hair.___
B
N.C.
Em

G
Gm7
A
(Spoken:) Indians scattered on dawn's highway bleeding ghosts crowd
E♭
C
G
the young child's fragile egg-shell mind.
Gm
C7
Gm
C7
Blood in the streets of the town of New Ha - ven;
Gm
C7
Gm
C7
Blood stains the roofs and the palm trees of Ven-ice.
Gm
C7
Gm
C7
Gm
C7
Blood in my love_ in the ter- ri-ble sum-mer;_ Blood-y red sun_ of fan -

Gm
C7
tas - tic L. A.
Blood screams her brain as they chop off her fin - gers.
Blood will be born in the birth of a na - tion;
Blood is the rose of mys-te - ri - ous un - ion.
3
D.S. al
There's
Fmaj7

Shaman's Blues

Words and Music by
JIM MORRISON

Copyright © 1969 Doors Music Co.
International Copyright Secured Made In U.S.A. All Rights Reserved

Cm
C
Will you give an-oth-er
chance?
Will you try a lit-tle
try?
loco
Gm
Please stop and you'll re-
mem-ber
we were to-
geth-er,
8va
F
an-y
way.
8va
loco
Gm
All
right
Gm
Now,
if you have a cert-ain
even-ing
you could lend
to me,
8va

I'll give it all right back to you. Know how it has to be
with you.
F
I know your moods
8va
loco
and your mind,
Gm
and your mind,
8va
and your mind,
and your mind,
and you'rc
mine.
8va
loco

Guitar Solo
Gm
F
3
Bb
D
Voice
Will you stop to think and won - der just what you'll see
3
3
8va
out on the train - yard nurs-ing pen- i - ten - tia - ry. It's
3
3
8va

Cm
gone. I cry out
loco
Gm
long.
8va
Gm
Did you stop_ to con- si - der how it will feel,
8va
cold grind-in' griz-zly bear jaws hot on your heels.
8va
Cm
Do you of- ten stop and whis - per in Sat - ur - day's shore (that) the
loco

whole world's a saviour, who could ev-er ev-er ev-er ev-er ev-er ev-er
8va
ask for more?
8va
Do you re-member?
loco
N.C.
Will you stop,
Gm N.C.
Gm
will you stop
p
the
N.C.
pain?
There will
Drums
p
f

*(Spoken ad lib over instrumental)
He's sweatin', look at him...optical promise...you'll be dead and in hell before I'm borne...sure thing...bridesmaid...the only solution--isn't it amazing?

Waiting For The Sun

Lyrics by JIM MORRISON
Music by THE DOORS

Copyright © 1970 Doors Music Co.
International Copyright Secured Made In U.S.A. All Rights Reserved

D7
G
Gm
Can't you feel it, now that spring has
N.C.
D7
G
come; that it's time to live in the
Gm
N.C.
scat - tered sun.
Eb F G
Eb F G
Eb F
Wait-ing for the sun, wait-ing for the sun, wait - ing for the
D
Eb F
G
sun, wait - ing for the sun.

Gm
B♭
F
Gm
Wait - ing,
wait - ing,
wait - ing,
wait - ing.
Gm
F
Gm
Wait - ing for you to
come a -
long;
F
Wait - ing for you to
hear my
Gm
song;
Wait-ing for you to
F
Gm
come a - long;

F
Gm
Wait-ing for you to tell me what went wrong.
F
This is the stran - gest
E♭
Dm
Gm
life I've ever known.
E♭
F
Wait - ing for the
Gm
N.C.
sun.

L'America

Lyrics by JIM MORRISON
Music by THE DOORS

Copyright © 1970 Doors Music Co.
International Copyright Secured Made In U.S.A. All Rights Reserved

Repeat ad lib
B
I took a trip down to l'A - mer - i - ca
B
to trade some beads for a pint of gold.
1.

2.
to
B
of gold.
B
l'A-mer- i - ca, l'A-mer- i - ca, l'A-mer - i - ca, l'A-mer -
1.
2.
B
E7
C'-mon, peo - ple, don't you
without 8va
E7
look so down; You know the rain-man's com-in' to town.
A7
A♯
He'll change your weath-er, he'll change your luck,

B N.C.
B
He'll e - ven teach you
how to
find your - self,
B
l'A - mer - i - ca.
(with 8va basso)
A
B♭
B
C
C♯
F♯ 7
B7

E
A
E
Friend-ly stran-gers came to town,
(without 8va basso)
A
E
A
all the peo-ple put them down.
But the wo-men
E
B
C
loved their ways
come a-gain some
oth-er
B
day.
Like the
gen-tle rain,
B
like the
gen-tle rain
that
falls.

B
(with 8va basso)
Repeat ad lib
B
Getting gradually faster
l'A-
mer - i - ca, l'A - mer - i - ca, l'A - mer - i - ca,
1.
2.
B
l'A -
l'A -
B
mer
- i - ca.
sfz

The End

Words and Music by
THE DOORS

Copyright © 1967 Doors Music Co.
International Copyright Secured Made In U.S.A. All Rights Reserved

D
C
G
D
stands, the end,
No
safe-ty
or
sur
-
prise, the end.
I'll
C
D
nev-er
look
in-to
your
eyes
a
-
gain.
cresc.
f
C
D
G7
Can you
pic-ture
what will
be,
So
lim
-
it
-
less
and
f
D
C
D
G
free,
des-p'rate-ly
in
need
of some
stran
-
ger's

D
C
D
hand, in a des-p'rate land.
D
Lost in a Ro-man wil-der-ness of
pain, and all the chil - dren
(piano continues to end)
are in - sane; all the chil-dren are in - sane;
wait-ing for the sum-mer rain. There's dan-ger on the

* The killer awoke before dawn,
He put his boots on,
He took a face from the ancient gallery,
And he walked on down the hall.

He went to the room where his sister lived,
And then he paid a visit to his brother,
And then he walked on down the hall.

And he came to a door,
And he looked inside,
"Father?"
"Yes, son?"
"I want to kill you.
"Mother, I want to...."

Come on, baby, take a chance with us, (3x)
And meet me at the back of the blue bus.

Runnin' Blues

Words and Music by
ROBBIE KRIEGER

Copyright © 1969 Doors Music Co.
International Copyright Secured Made In U.S.A. All Rights Reserved

Voice
Piano
(spoken)
D A E7 A D A E7 A7
All right, look at my shoes, not quite the walk - in' blues.
D A E7 A D A E7
Don't fight, too much to lose. Can't fight the Run - nin' Blues.
Am
Am G Am
Well, I've got the Run - nin' Blues

Am G Bm A C
Run-nin' a-way, back to L. A. Got to find the
Bm A C Bm A
dock on the bay may-be find it back in L. A.
Am7 Cm7 Am7 C dim Am7 Cdim Am7 Cdim Am Cm Am Cdim
Run-nin' scared, Run-nin' Blue,
Am Cm Am F♯m Em6/9 Am
go-in' so fast, what'll I do?
D A
(spoken)
E7 A D A E7 A
All right, look at my shoes, not quite the walk - in' blues,
Voice
Piano

1.
D
A
E7
A
D
A
E7
don't fight, too much to lose; Can't fight the Run - nin' Blues.
2.
E
A7
Dm
Am
E7
A7
Dm
Am
E7
A7
Dm
Am
E7
A7
Dm
Am
E
A

Wishful Sinful

Words and Music by
ROBBIE KRIEGER

Wishful Sinful - 3 - 1

Copyright © 1968, 1969 Doors Music Co.
International Copyright Secured Made In U.S.A. All Rights Reserved

C E A D F C
Wish - ful sin - ful wick-ed blue wa - ter cov - ers
D C E A D
you. Wish-ful sin - ful wick-ed you,
F C D
can't es- cape the blue.
D Bb(5) Bm
Mag-ic ris-ing sun is shin-ing, deep be-neath the
Bb A D Am
sea. But, not en-ough for you and me and sun-shine.

D
Am
D
Love to hear the wind cry.
D
D.S. al
D
Am
D
You and me and sun - shine,
love to
Am
D
Am
hear the wind
D
Am
D
cry.

Twentieth Century Fox

Words and Music by
THE DOORS

Copyright © 1966 Doors Music Co.
International Copyright Secured Made In U.S.A. All Rights Reserved

A
E7
A
E7
A
Twen-ti-eth
Cen-tu-ry Fox,_ She's a
Twen-ti-eth
Cen-tu-ry Fox;_ No
Got the
Am
G
F
C
tears, no fears, no ru-ined_ years, no
world locked up in - side a plas - tic
E
E7
A
D
A
E7
clocks; She's a Twen-ti-eth Cen-tu-ry Fox.
box;
A G A G A G A G
5
3
5
3
3
3

A G F D E9 E9♮
A G A G A G F D E7 D.S. to ⊕
She's the
A D A D A D A D
Twen-ti-eth Cen-tu-ry Fox, yeh.
A D A D A Em7 A
Twen-ti-eth Cen-tu-ry Fox.
3
3

Spanish Caravan

Words and Music by
THE DOORS

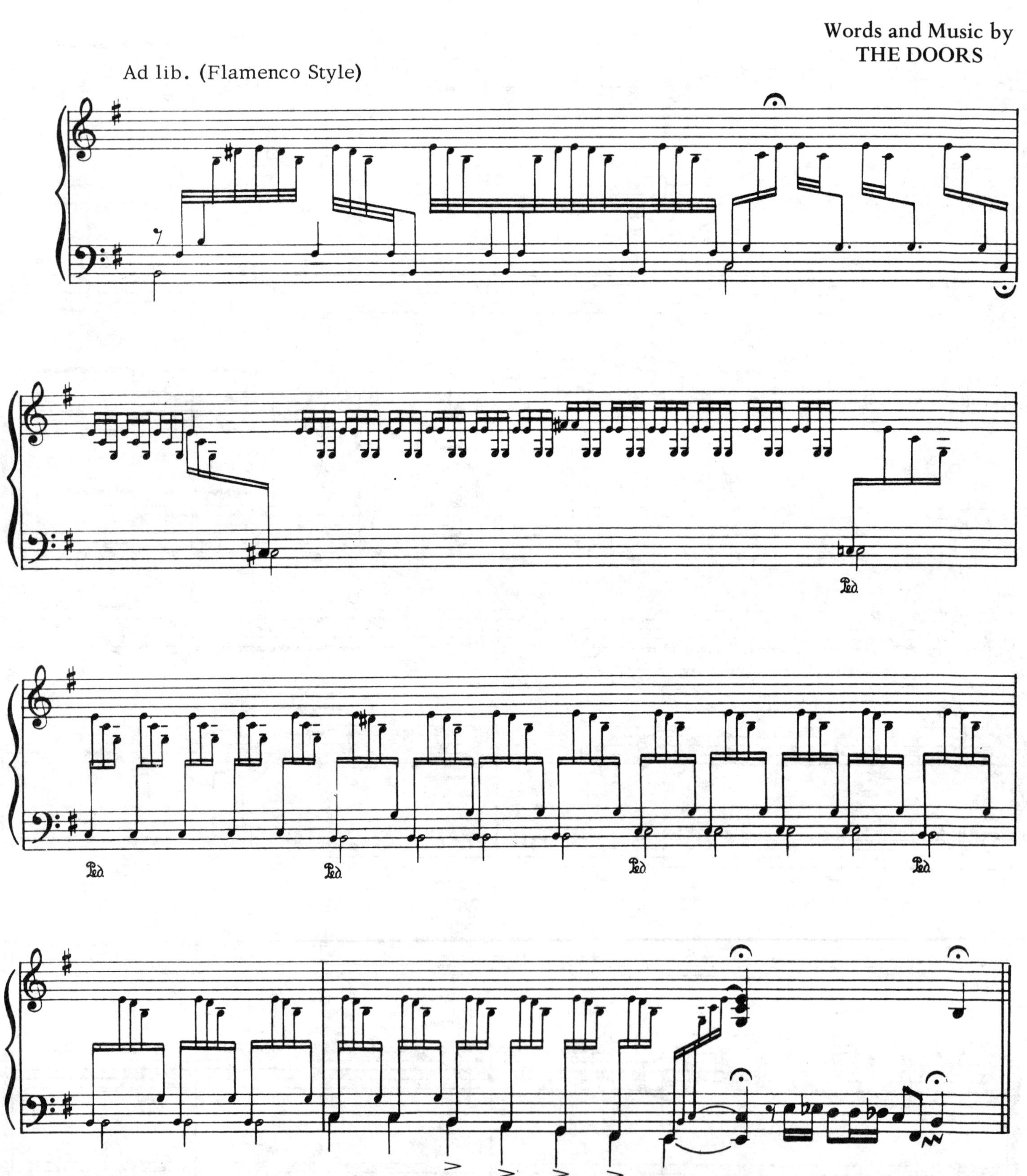

Copyright © 1968 Doors Music Co.
International Copyright Secured Made In U.S.A. All Rights Reserved

Allegro (in 1)
tacet
B
C 7
B

A
D
G
C
F
Bb
F#
B
Much Slower (in 3)
Em
Am
B
Em
Carry me, caravan, take me away,
Take me to
Am
B
Em
Am
Em
Portugal, take me to Spain,
Andalusia, with

B7
Em
Am
Em
B7
fields full of grain, I have to see you a - gain and a -
Em
D7
gain. Take me, Span - ish Car - a - van, Yes, I
C
ad lib
(long)
B7
know you can.
(long)
Very fast (in 1)
(tacet)
f

8va
B
8va
C7
8va
B
8va
loco
A
D

G
C
F
B♭
F♯
B
C
(long)
Em7
ff
(long)

Hyacinth House

Lyrics by JIM MORRISON
Music by THE DOORS

Copyright © 1971 Doors Music Co.
International Copyright Secured Made In U.S.A. All Rights Reserved

D
Am
G
Hy - a-cinth House _ to please the
li-ons _
this
D
day?
I
need
a
D
brand new _ friend _ who does-n't
both-er
me, _
D
I
need
a
brand new _ friend _ who does - n't
trou-ble
me. _
D
Am
G
I
need
some-one _
who,
who
does - n't

F D
D♯m Em
need me.
I see the
Em
bath-room is clear,
I think that
some-bod-y's near,
Em
F♯m
I'm sure that
some-one is fol - low-ing
me.
F♯m
G
A7 N.C.
Oh,
yeah.
D
Why did you throw the Jack - of - Hearts a - way?

D
Why did you throw the Jack - of - Hearts _ a - way? _ It was the
Am
G
D
on - ly card _ in the deck that I _ had left to play. _
D
And I'll
Am
G
1. 2.
D
say it a - gain, _ I need a brand new friend,
D
And I'll
3.
D7
G
D
G
D
brand new friend, _ the end. _

Changeling

Lyrics by JIM MORRISON
Music by THE DOORS

Bright Rock Beat

Copyright © 1971 Doors Music Co.
International Copyright Secured Made In U.S.A. All Rights Reserved

A7 (+9)
A7 (+9)
I live
A7 (+9)
up town,
I live
down - town,
I live
all a-round.
I had
mon - ey,

A7 (+9)
I had none;
I had
A7 (+9)
mon - ey,
I had none;
A7 (+9)
But I
Am
nev - er been so broke that I
could - n't leave
Am
town.
I'm a
change - ling
Am
see me change.
I'm a

Am
change - ling
see me change.
Am
Am
I'm the
air you breathe,
food you eat,
Am
(Orch.)
F
friends you greet in the swarm-ing street.
F
See me
to 2nd Coda
Am
change,
see me change.

Am
I live
Coda
A sus4
A9
town.
I'm the
Second Coda
Am
I'm leav-ing town
on the mid-night train
Am
gon-na see me change,
Am
change, change,
change,
change, change.
(Repeat and fade)

You're Lost, Little Girl

Words and Music by
THE DOORS

Copyright © 1967 Doors Music Co.
International Copyright Secured Made In U.S.A. All Rights Reserved

D
Gm
D
Gm
Think that you
know what to
do,
Im-
D
Gm
D
pos - si-ble
yes, but it's
true,
G
Bm
I
think that you
know what to
F
A
D
do,
Yeah,
sure that you
Gm
D
know what to
do.
You're

Em
C
Em
lost,
lit - tle
girl,
C
Em
C
You're
lost,
lit - tle
girl,
Em
C
Em
You're
lost,
tell me
C
G
F
A
who
are
you.
Em
C
poco rit.
Em
You're
lost.

We Could Be So Good Together

Words and Music by
THE DOORS

Copyright © 1968 Doors Music Co.
International Copyright Secured Made In U.S.A. All Rights Reserved

Am
Ab
G
Ab
Tell you lies, I'll tell you wicked lies,
Am
Ab
G
G#m
Am
Tell you lies, Tell you wick-ed lies.
D
G
G#
A
D
A
D
G#
I tell you 'bout the world that we'll in - vent, Wan - ton world with-
A
D
A
G
Am
out la-ment, en - ter-prise, ex - pe-di - tion, in - vi - ta-tion and in-ven-tion.
Am
Yeah, so good to-geth - er, ah, so good to-geth - er, We could be so

A
good to-geth - er,
Yeh, we could,
know we could.__
G
A N.C.
We could be so
good to-geth-er,
Yeh, so
good to-geth - er,
We could be so
good to geth - er,
Yeh, we could,
know we could.__
Bm7
E7(b5)
A7
Bb
Tell
you lies,___
Tell you wick-ed lies,___

Bm7
E7(♭5)
A
B♭
B7
Tell you lies,
Tell you wick-ed lies.
The
E
A
E
B
E
B
E
A
E
B
E
B
time you wait sub-tracts from joy,
Be-heads the an-gels
you de-stroy;
A
B
N.C.
An-gels fight,
An-gels cry;
An-gels dance and
An-gels die.
Bm
Am
B♭
B♭m

Strange Days

Words and Music by
THE DOORS

Copyright © 1967 Doors Music Co.
International Copyright Secured Made In U.S.A. All Rights Reserved

F#
G
Cm
down, They're goin' to de-
Gm
Cm
Gm
stroy our cas-
Cm
Gm
u - al joys, We
G
B
B♭
shall go on play - ing or find
F
E
a new town.

G
B
B♭
F
G
B
B♭
F
Em
Em
Strange
Am
Em
Am
eyes
fill
strange
rooms,
Em
Am
Em
voic - es
will
sig - nal
their
ti - red
F♯
G
end,
The
host -

Strange days have found us
And through their strange hours
We linger alone,
Bodies confused,
Memories misused,
As we run from the day
To a strange night of stone.

Love Me Two Times

Words and Music by
THE DOORS

* play ♩♩♩♩ as ♩♪ ♩♪ (triplets)

Copyright © 1967 Doors Music Co.
International Copyright Secured Made In U.S.A. All Rights Reserved

Fm
Fm
I'm goin' a - way.
Love me two times, girl,
Eb
One for to-mor-row,
one just for to-day;
Db
Ab
Eb
Db7
Fm
Love me two times,
I'm goin' a-way.
Fm

Fm
Love me one time,
Could not
speak;
Bb7
Love me one time,
Yeh, my knee got
Fm
weak.
Fm
Love me two times, girl,
Eb
Last me
all thru the week;
Db

Ab
Eb
Db7
Fm
Love me two times,
I'm goin' a - way;
Fm
Ab
Eb
Db7
Love me two times,
I'm goin' a - way.
Fm
Ab
Eb
Love me two times,
Db7
Fm
I'm goin' a - way.

People Are Strange

Words and Music by
THE DOORS

Copyright © 1967 Doors Music Co.
International Copyright Secured Made In U.S.A. All Rights Reserved

1. 3.
C7
Ab
Bbm7
C7
No one re-mem-bers your name
when you're strange
1. 3.
(to 3rd ending)
when you're strange
when you're strange.
2.
C7
Fm
C7
Fm
Bbm Bdim C Fm6 F# dim C Fm
Fm7
when you're down.
2.
D dim
Db
C7
Fm
3.
rall.
C7
when you're
strange.
rall.
arp.

The Crystal Ship

Copyright © 1967 Doors Music Co.
International Copyright Secured Made In U.S.A. All Rights Reserved

F
Eb
F
Eb
1. 3.
F
Db
Ab
Eb
1. bliss, an - oth - er kiss, (kiss,) an - oth - er kiss.
2. sane, we'll meet a - gain, (gain,) we'll meet — a -
3. why you'd rath - er cry, (cry) I'd rath - er fly.
C7
2.
F
2. The gain.
4. The
Fm
Eb
Fm
Eb
Fm
Db
Ab
Eb
C7
D.S.
3. oh,
Coda
F
Eb
F
rall.
Eb
time; when we get back, — I'll — drop a line. —
rall.

The Unknown Soldier

Words and Music by
THE DOORS

Copyright © 1968 Doors Music Co.
International Copyright Secured Made In U.S.A. All Rights Reserved

Ab
G
G#
ver for the un-known sol - dier,
A
Ab
G
it's all o - ver for the un-known sol-
G#
Am
dier uh uh
chant over military drum
(spoken)
"Company
halt!"
"Present Arms"
(Military Drum Roll)
Gun Shot)
R.H.
L.H.

(repeat and fade)

Ship Of Fools

Lyrics by JIM MORRISON
Music by THE DOORS

Copyright © 1970 Doors Music Co.
International Copyright Secured Made In U.S.A. All Rights Reserved

Bm
Yeah,
A - long came Mis - ter Good -
trips
look - ing for a new ship.
Come on, peo - ple, bet - ter
climb on board;
Come on, ba - by, now we're
go - ing home.
Ship of
fools,
Ship of
fools,

Dm
D.S. 𝄋 to 𝄌
G
Bm
E7
A7
(no repeat)
𝄌 E7
A7
D
Am
D
Smog will get you pretty soon.
Ship of fools,
D
Ship of fools,
Ship of fools,
Repeat and fade

Moonlight Drive

Words and Music by
THE DOORS

Copyright © 1967 Doors Music Co.
International Copyright Secured Made In U.S.A. All Rights Reserved

A♭7
moon - light drive
A7
Let's swim to the moon uh huh Let's climb thru the tide,
sur - ren - der to the wait - ing worlds that
E7
lap a - gainst our side noth - in' left o - pen and no
A7
time to de - cide we've stepped in - to a riv - er on our

A
D
A7
D
moon light drive
Let's swim to the
moon
Let's climb thru the
tide
You reach a hand to hold me but I
can't be your guide
E7
eas - y to
love you as I
watch you glide
fall - ing through wet
for - ests on our
moon-light drive.
(repeat and fade)

L.A. Woman

Words and Music by
THE DOORS

Bright beat

Copyright © 1971 Doors Music Co.
International Copyright Secured Made In U.S.A. All Rights Reserved

A
A
Well, I
A
just got in-to town a-bout an hour a-go
A
took a look a-round, see which way the wind blow,
A
Where the lit-tle girls in their

A
Hol - ly-wood bun - ga - lows,
Are you a
A
luck-y lit - tle la - dy in the ci - ty of light?
A
or just an - oth - er lost an - gel.
Ci - ty of night,
G
G#
A
ci - ty of night,
A
G
G#
ci - ty of night,
ci - ty of night.

A
A
L. A. wo - man,
L. A. wo - man,
A
L. A. wo - man, Sun - day af - ter - noon,
A
L. A. wo - man, Sun - day
A
af - ter - noon,

A
L. A. wo - man, Sun-day af - ter-noon
drive thru your sub-urbs
A G G♯
in-to your blues,
in-to your
A G
blues,
in-to your blue, blue, blues,
G G♯ A
in-to your blues.
A G A G A G

A G A G A G
I see your hair is burn - ing
A G A G A G
hills are filled with
A G A G A G
fi - re;
If they
A G A G A G
say I nev - er loved you
A G A G A G
you know they are a li - ar.

A G A G A G
Driv - in' down the
A G A G A G
free - way
A G A G A G
mid - night al - leys roam
A G A
Cops in cars, the top - less bars,
A
nev - er saw a wo - man so a -

G
G♯
A
lone, so a - lone,
A
G
G♯
so a - lone, so a - lone.
A
Mo - tel mon-ey
A
mur - der mad - ness
A
let's change the mood from glad to sad - ness.

Double tempo (slow 4)
Am
Am
Mis - ter
Am
Mo - jo ris - in' Mis - ter Mo - jo ris - in' Mis - ter
Am
(Getting gradually faster and faster)
Mo - jo ris - in' Mis - ter Mo - jo ris - in' got to
Am
keep on ris - in' Mis - ter Mo - jo ris - in' Mis - ter

Faster
Am
Mo - jo ris - in'
Mo - jo ris - in'
Mis - ter
Am
Mo - jo ris - in'
Mis - ter
Faster
Mo - jo ris - in'
got to
Am
keep on ris - in'
ris - in', ris - in',
Am
ris in', ris - in',
ris - in', ris - in',
ris - in', ris - in',
ris - in', ris - in',

Tempo I
A
A
G
G♯
ci - ty of night,
ci - ty of night.
A
A
A
A
L. A. wo - man,
she's my wo - man,
L. A. wo - man.
L. A. wo - man.
Repeat and fade

Take It As It Comes

Words and Music by
THE DOORS

Copyright © 1966 Doors Music Co.
International Copyright Secured Made In U.S.A. All Rights Reserved

Am F E Am F E
mov- in' much too fast.
(Solo)
Am F E Am F E
Am F E
1. Am
2. Am F E Am F E

Am
F
E
Am
F
E
Go real slow, You'll like it more and more,
Am
F
E
Am
F
E
(to Chorus)
Take it as it comes. Spe-cial - ize in hav - in' fun.
Coda
Am
F
E
Am
F
E
mov - in' much too fast, Mov-in' much too fast,
Am
F
Am
Mov - in' much too fast.

Wintertime Love

Words and Music by
THE DOORS

Copyright © 1968 Doors Music Co.
International Copyright Secured Made In U.S.A. All Rights Reserved

B♭
A
E
A
hands touch - ing me.
ly to be free.
G
D
D7
Come with me, dance, my dear,
F♯
Bm
Am
Win - ter's so cold this year.
G
A
G
A
You are so warm, my Win - ter - time Love to
D
A
E
A
be.

Bm
F♯7
A7
E7
A
E
A
gliss.
D
A rit.
D
be.

Soul Kitchen

Words and Music by
THE DOORS

Copyright © 1966 Doors Music Co.
International Copyright Secured Made In U.S.A. All Rights Reserved

A D7 A D7 A D7
night. The cars crawl past all
A D7 A D7 A D7
stuffed with eyes, Street lights shed their hol-low glow; your
A D7 A D7 A D7
brain seems bruised with numb sur-prise Still one place to
A D7 A D7 A D7
go, Still one place to go. Let me
f

Chorus
Em D7 Em D7 Em D7
sleep all night in your soul kit-chen, warm my mind near
Em D7 Em D7 Em D
your gentle stove. Turn me out and I'll wan - der, ba - by,
E7 A D6 A D6
stum-bling in the ne-on groves. Your fin-gers weave quick mi - na - rets,
A D6 A D6 A D6 A D6
speak-ing in se - cret al-pha - bets. I light an - oth-er ci-ga - rette,

Am
D
A
D6
Am
D
A
D6
Learn to for - get,
Learn to for - get,
A
D6
A
D6
Am
D
1. A
D6
2. A
D6
Learn to for - get,
Learn to for - get
get
D.C. to ⊕
A
D7
A
D7
A
D7
night
all ___ night.
A
D7
A
All
night. ___

Roadhouse Blues

Lyrics by JIM MORRISON
Music by THE DOORS

Copyright © 1970 Doors Music Co.
International Copyright Secured Made In U.S.A. All Rights Reserved

Piano
E
A
a good time.
E
A
E
A
E
Yeah, in
E
back of the road-house they got some bun-ga lows
1.
Yeah, in
2.
And
that's for the peo - ple who
like to go down
slow.
Let it

A
1.2.
E
3.
A7
roll ___ ba - by, roll; ___ let it
Yeah, let it
Repeat 3 times
B7
C7
B7
E
E
roll, ___
all night
long.
E7
Ash-en la - dy,
Ash-en la - dy,
give
up your
vow!
Give
up your
vow! ___
Save our
cit - y,

Save our cit-y,
right
now!
When I
E
woke up this morn - in' I
got my - self a beer.
1.
When I
2.
The
fu-ture is un-cer-tain and the end is al - ways
near.
Let it
B7 C7
C#7 D7 Eb7 E
N.C.
E E9
all night
long.

Land Ho!

Lyrics by JIM MORRISON
Music by THE DOORS

Copyright © 1970 Doors Music Co.
International Copyright Secured Made In U.S.A. All Rights Reserved

from liv - in' on the land.
and old time lib - er - ty,
Got to find my ship-mates and walk on for - eign sands."
Songs of love and songs of death, and songs to set men free.
C
A
D
C
A
G
1.
F♯m
Em
A7
2.
F♯m
Em

Dm
Em
Dm
I've
Em
Dm
Em
Dm
got three ships and six - ty men, a
Stand at mast, let north winds blow till
Em
Dm
1.
Em
D
course for ports un - read.
half of us are
2.
Em
D
dead.
(shouted:)
Land Ho!
(Drums)
Well, if I

D
get my hands on a dol-lar bill, gon-na buy a bot-tle and
get my hands on a num ber five, gon-na skin that lit-tle
1.
2.
drink my fill. If I girl a-live. If I get my hands on a
num - ber two come back home and mar - ry you,
mar - ry you, mar - ry you. All right!
D
Land Ho!
Repeat and fade

End Of The Night

Words and Music by
THE DOORS

Copyright © 1966 Doors Music Co.
International Copyright Secured Made In U.S.A. All Rights Reserved

Am
Em
Am
Em
Some are born to sweet de-light.
Some are born to sweet de-light.
F♯7
B7
Em
D
D♯m
Em
Some are born to the end-less night.
End of the night
3
D
D♯m
Em
End of the night
End of the night
End of the night
Fine
Am
Em
Am
Em
Am
Em
F♯7
B7
Em
D
D♯m Em
D
D♯m Em
D.S. al Fine

Cars Hiss By My Window

Lyrics by JIM MORRISON
Music by THE DOORS

Slow Blues Beat

Copyright © 1971 Doors Music Co.
International Copyright Secured Made In U.S.A. All Rights Reserved

E
B7
I got this girl be-side me, but she's
A7
E
out of reach.
E
Head-lights thru my win-dow
shin-ing on the wall
E
A7
Head-lights thru my win-dow
climb-ing on the wall,

E
B7
Can't hear my ba - by
A7
tho' I call and call.
E
E
B
E
E
A7
Win - dow starts to trem - ble
with a son - ic boom.

E
A7
Win - dow starts to trem-ble
with a son - ic boom.
E
A
B7
Cold girl will kill you
A7
in a dark - ened room.
E
Am6
Bbm6 E9
rit.

Yes The River Knows

Words and Music by
THE DOORS

Copyright © 1968 Doors Music Co.
International Copyright Secured Made In U.S.A. All Rights Reserved

E Dm C E Am G F E
Free fall flow riv-er, flow on and on it goes
E Dm C E Am G Am Bm E Dm
Breathe un-der wa-ter till the end. Free fall
F G Am G F E Am G7
flow riv-er flow on and on it goes, Breathe un - der
Am E7
to continue
to finish.
Fine
wa-ter till the end. Yes the riv-er knows. end.
poco rit.

Emaj7
Dmaj7
Emaj7
Dmaj7
Please be - lieve me, If you don't need me I'm
F♯m
B4sus
B7
go - ing but I need a lit-tle time, I
F♯m
C♯m
G♯m
C♯m
prom-ised I would drown my - self in mys - tic heat-ed wine.

A
F
Please be - lieve me___ the riv - er told me___
B♯
B♯m
ver - y soft - ly want you to
F♯
hold me.
Emaj7
Dmaj7

G♯m
F♯m7
Emaj7
3
Dmaj7
3
G♯m
B♯m
Em
Bm
E7
Voice
I'm
F♯m
B4sus
B7
go - ing but I need a lit-tle time, I
F♯m
C♯m
G♯m
C♯m
D.S. al Fine
prom-ised I would drown my-self in mys-tic heat-ed wine.
poco rall.

Touch Me

Words and Music by
THE DOORS

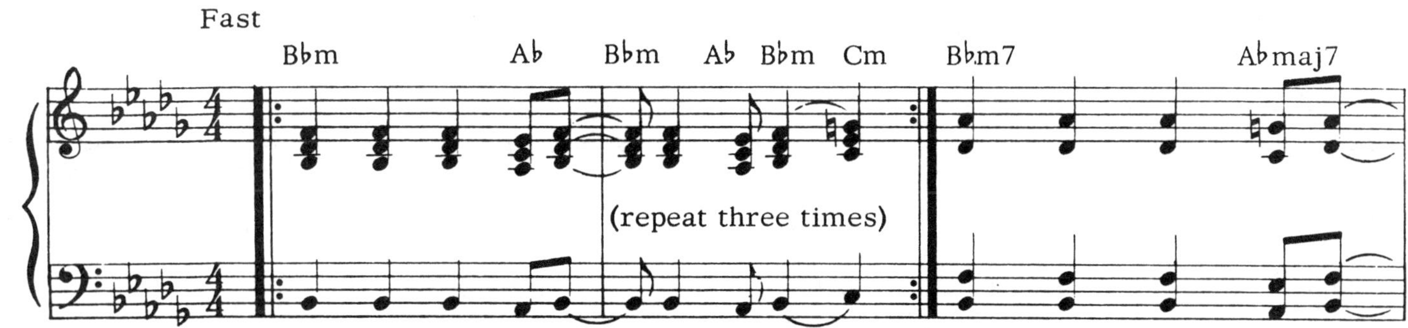

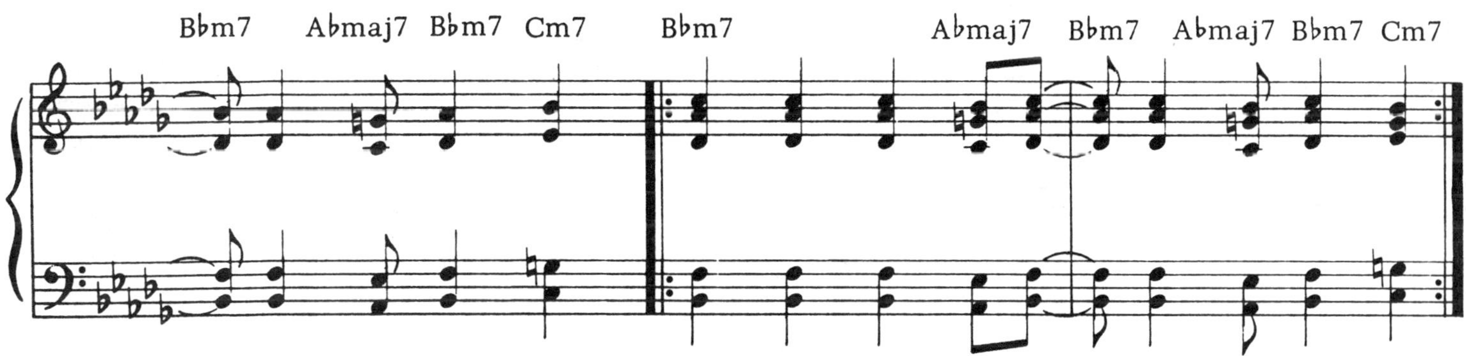

Copyright © 1968, 1969 Doors Music Co.
International Copyright Secured Made In U.S.A. All Rights Reserved

Fb
Cb
What was that
prom-ise that you made,
Ebm
Ebm7
E
G
Why won't you
tell me what she said,
D
What was that
prom-ise that she made
Now
G
F#m
G
I'm
gon-na
love you
till the
heav - en
A
D
G
stops
the
rain
I'm
gon-na
F#m
G
A
G
A6
A9
love
you
till the
stars
fall
from
the
sky
for you and

D
Da Capo
I.
Softly
G
F♯m
G
I'm
gon-na
love you
till the
heav- en
A
D
G
stops
the
rain,
I'm
gon - na
F♯m
G
A
G
love
you
till the
stars
fall
from
the
sky,
f
Em7
A7
D
for
you and
I.
ff
D
fff

Not To Touch The Earth

Words and Music by
THE DOORS

Copyright © 1968 Doors Music Co.
International Copyright Secured Made In U.S.A. All Rights Reserved

Dm
Cm6
Dm
Cm6
Dm
Cm6
House up-on the hill,
Moon is ly-ing still,
Sha-dows of the trees,

Dm
Cm6
Dm
Cm6
Dm
Cm6
Dm
wit-ness-ing the wild breeze. Come on, Ba-by, run with me, Let's run
Drums

Gm
Fm
run with me,
run with me,

Gm
D
run with me
Let's
run.

Em Dm6 Em Dm6 Em Dm6 Em Dm6
Voice
The

Em Dm6 Em Dm6 Em Dm6 Em Dm6
man-sion is warm at the top of the hill,
Rich are the rooms and the com-forts there

Em Dm6 Em Dm6 Em Dm6 Em Dm6
Red are the arms of lux - u - ri-ant chairs, And you don't know a thing till you get in-side

Voice
Orchestra
Dead

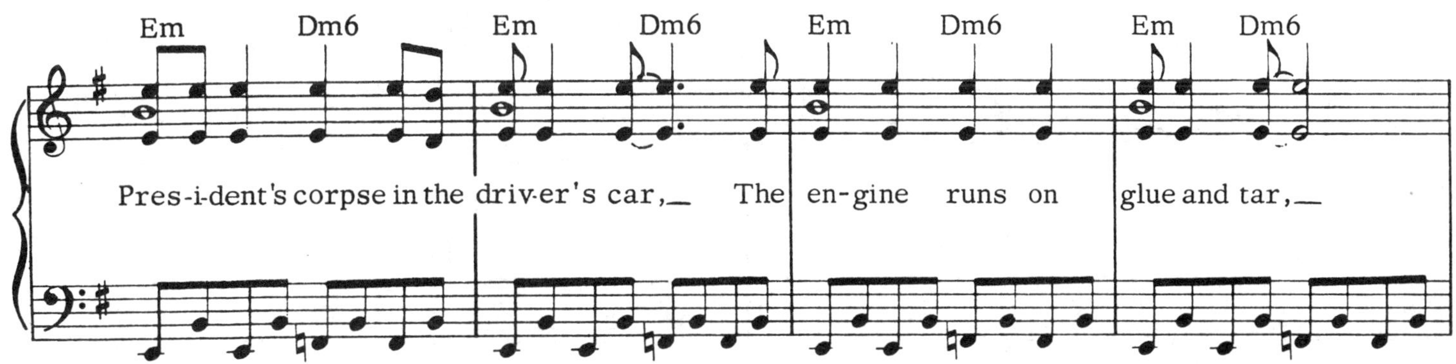
Em
Dm6
Em
Dm6
Em
Dm6
Em
Dm6
Pres-i-dent's corpse in the driv-er's car,
The en-gine runs on glue and tar,

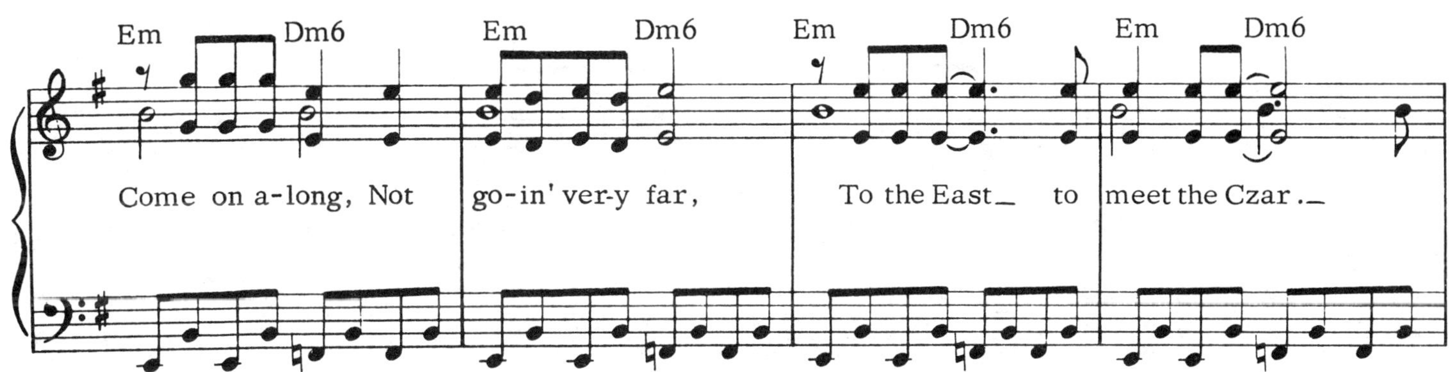
Em
Dm6
Em
Dm6
Em
Dm6
Em
Dm6
Come on a-long, Not go-in' ver-y far,
To the East to meet the Czar.

Em
Am
Gm
Run with me,
Run with me,

Am
E
Run with me.
Let's run.

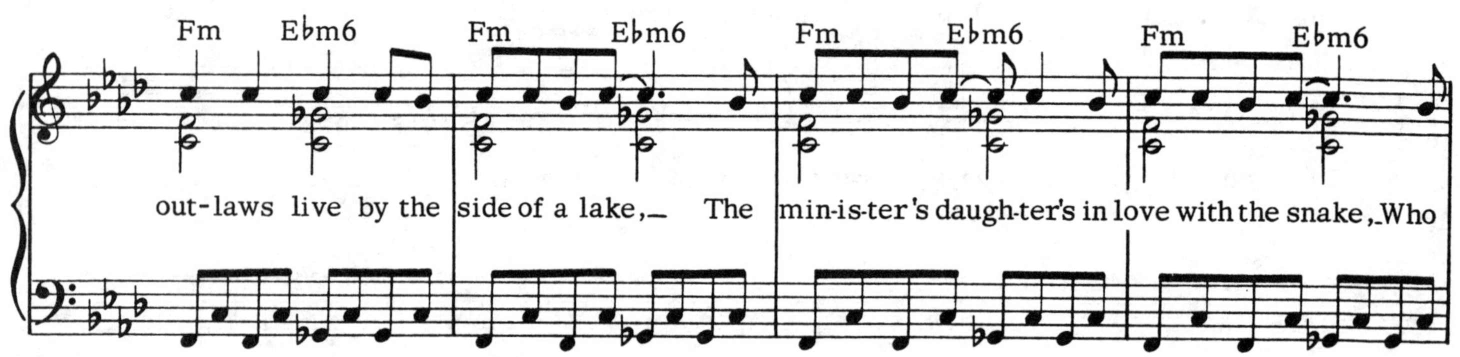

(repeat ad lib)

I Can't See Your Face

Words and Music by
THE DOORS

Copyright © 1967 Doors Music Co.
International Copyright Secured Made In U.S.A. All Rights Reserved

Am
Dm
C♯m7
Don't you cry,
E♭maj7
Gm7
ba - by, please don't cry,
Gm' G♯m
Am
E7
and don't look at me with your eyes,
Am
E7
A sus4
I can't seem to
G sus4
A sus4
G sus4
find the right lie, I

A sus4
G sus4
A sus4
G sus4
can't seem to find the right lie. In-
E7
A7
san - i-ty's horse a - dorns the sky,
Dm7
E7
Am
E7
can't seem to find the right lie,
Gm
G♯m
Am
E7
I won't need your pic - ture
A sus4
G sus4
A sus4
L.H.
un-til we say good - bye.

The Wasp

Lyrics by JIM MORRISON
Music by THE DOORS

Copyright © 1971 Doors Music Co.
International Copyright Secured Made In U.S.A. All Rights Reserved

Em
some call it heavenly in its brilliance
others, mean and rueful of the Western dream
I love the friends I have gathered together on this thin raft
we have constructed pyramids in honor of our escaping.
(repeat ad lib)
This is the land where the Pharaoh died.
E
F♯
E
F♯
G
E
F♯
E
F♯
A
A♯
B
E
F♯
E
F♯
E
F♯
G♯
G
F♯
E
Em

Em
The Negroes in the
forest, brightly feathered,
and they are saying:
Em
"Forget the night!
live with us in forests of azure,
out here on the perimeter, there are no stars.
Out here we is stoned - immaculate."
E
F#
E
F#
G
(Sung:)
1. Lis-ten to this I'll tell you a - bout the heart - aches; I'll
2. Lis-ten to this I'll tell you a - bout Tex - as; I'll
E
F#
E
F#
A
A#
B
tell you a - bout the heart - ache and the loss of God. I'll
tell you a - bout Tex - as Ra - di - o. I'll

E F♯ E F♯ C♯ A C♯ A
tell you a-bout the hope-less night, the mea - ger food my soul for - got,
tell you a-bout the hope-less night, the wan - der - in' the West - ern dream,
F♯ G♯ G F♯ E Em
tell you a - bout the maid-en with wrought i - ron soul.
Em
(spoken) I want to tell you about Texas Radio and the big beat,
Em
soft-driven, slow and mad
like some new language.
G♯ G F♯ E
wrought i - ron soul.

Five To One

Words and Music by
THE DOORS

Copyright © 1968 Doors Music Co.
International Copyright Secured Made In U.S.A. All Rights Reserved

Am G Am G Am G
old get old — and the young get strong - er, May take a week and it
(repeat pattern till piano Solo)
Am G Am G Am G
may take long - er, They got the guns but we got the num-bers.
Am tacet
Gon-na win, yeh, we're tak-in' o - ver, come on.
Am
(Solo)

Your ball-room days are o - ver, ba - by, Night is draw - ing near,
Sha-dows of the eve - ning grow a - cross the year.

(repeat and fade)

Maggie M'Gill

Lyrics by JIM MORRISON
Music by THE DOORS

Copyright © 1970 Doors Music Co.
International Copyright Secured Made In U.S.A. All Rights Reserved

Am

Now, if you're sad and you're

8va b.

Am

feel-in' blue,__ Go out and buy a brand new pair of shoes, And

8va

Dm

you go down,__ down to "Tan - gie Town."__

Am

The

C

peo-ple down there__

D

real-ly like to__ get it on,__

Am

get it on.__

8va b.

Am

8va

Am
Il - le - gi - ti - mate son of a rock
and roll star.
1.
Il - le -
2.
Mom met Dad in the back of a rock 'n roll car.
Yeah.
Well, I'm an old blues man and I think that you
8va

Am
under stand.
I've been
8va
Am
sing-ing the blues
ev - er since the world be - gan.
8va
Am
8va
Am
Mag - gie, Mag - gie, Mag-gie M'-Gill,
8va
Am
roll on, roll on, Mag-gie M' - Gill.
8va
Repeat and fade

Summer's Almost Gone

Words and Music by
THE DOORS

Copyright © 1968 Doors Music Co.
International Copyright Secured Made In U.S.A. All Rights Reserved

Ab Eb Db Bb Cm
Morn-ing found us calm-ly un-a - ware,
Eb Db Ab G7
Noon burned gold in - to our hair,
At night

Fm7 Eb Db Cm
we swam the laugh-ing sea.
When sum-mer's gone,

G7 Fm Cm Bb
1.
where will we be?
where will we be

Cm
where will we be?
2.
Cm
Cm
B♭
Cm
Sum-mer's al-most gone,
Sum-mer's al-most gone
Cm
B♭
Cm
B♭
Fm7
Cm
B♭
We had some
good times
but they're gone.
Cm
G7
Fm
Cm
The
win-ter's com-ing on,
sum-mer's al-most
gone.

Queen Of The Highway

Medium Rock

Words and Music by
JIM MORRISON and
ROBBIE KRIEGER

Queen Of The Highway - 3 - 1

Copyright © 1970 Doors Music Co.
International Copyright Secured Made In U.S.A. All Rights Reserved

F♯
her,
dren,
save the blind ti - ger.
wild as can be,
Gm
Cm7
He was a mon - ster, black dressed in leath-er.
Soon to have off - spring, start it all o - ver.
1.
Gm
F
She was a prin - cess, Queen of the High -
way.
B
2.
Gm
F
N.C.
Start it all o - ver.

3. American boy, American girl,
Most beautiful people in the world!
Son of a frontier Indian Swirl,
Dancing thru the midnight whirl-pool
Formless hope it can
continue a little longer.

Easy Ride

Words and Music by
JIM MORRISON

Copyright © 1969 Doors Music Co.
International Copyright Secured Made In U.S.A. All Rights Reserved

F
C7
The mask that you wore my fing - ers would ex -
F
plore cos - tume of con - trol ex -
F#
G
cite - ment soon un - folds
G
G7
And I know it will
C7
be an Eas - y Ride,

G7
yeah,
joy
fought
vague - ly
with your
pride
with your
pride
Fm
Eb
Db

G
G7
G7
N.C.
G7
C7

(repeat and fade)

Unhappy Girl

Words and Music by
THE DOORS

Copyright © 1967 Doors Music Co.
International Copyright Secured Made In U.S.A. All Rights Reserved

1.
2.
Cm
Bb
Cm
Bb
Cm
in a pris - on of your
in a pris - own de - vice. And you
in a pris -
Gm
Fm
Bbm7
can't be - lieve what it does to me to
Cm
see you cry - in'.
Bb
Cm
- on of your own de - vice.

Bb
Cm
Bb
Cm
Ab
Cm
G7
Cm
3.
Bb
Cm
ritard.
Bb
Cm
- on
of your
own __ de - vice.
ritard.

Blue Sunday

Words and Music by
JIM MORRISON

Copyright © 1970 Doors Music Co.
International Copyright Secured Made In U.S.A. All Rights Reserved

Bb C Db C
F
3
Now I have found my girl. My

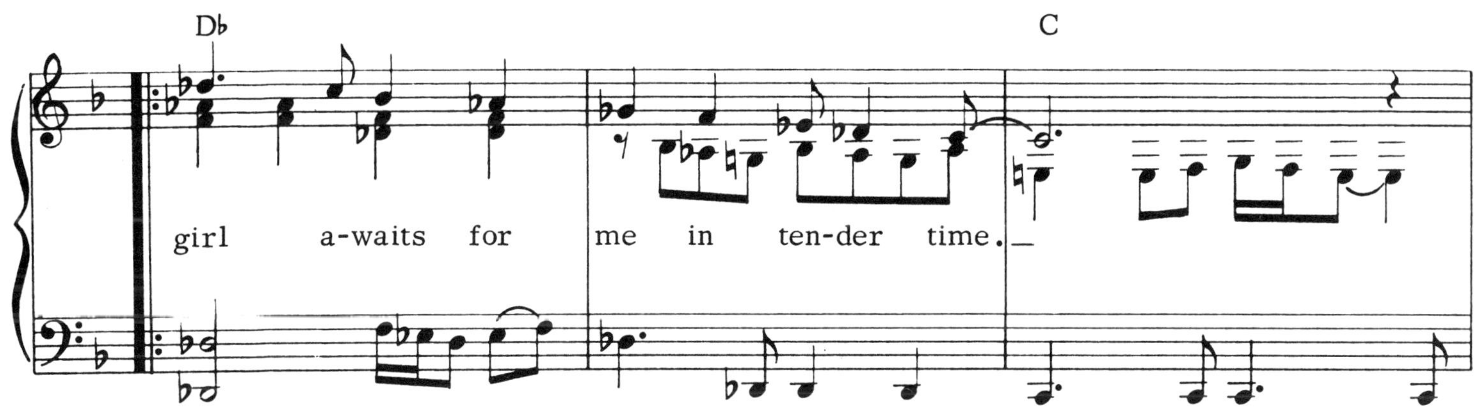
Db
C
girl a-waits for me in ten-der time.

Bb C Db C
Bb C Db C
F Db
3
My girl is mine, She is the world, she is my

1.
2.
F
F
girl. My girl.

My Wild Love

Words and Music by
THE DOORS

My wild love went riding,
She rode all the day;
She rode to the devil,
And asked him to pay.

The devil was wiser.
It's time to repent;
He asked her to give back,
The money he spent.

My wild love went riding,
She rode to sea;
She gathered together
Some shells for her hair.

She rode on to Christmas,
She rode to the farm;
She rode to Japan
And re-entered a town.

My wild love is crazy
She screams like a bird;
She moans like a cat
When she wants to be heard.

She rode and she rode on
She rode for a while,
Then stopped for an evening
And laid her head down.

By this time the weather
Had changed one degree,
She asked for the people
To let her go free.

My wild love went riding,
She rode for an hour;
She stopped and she rested,
And then she rode on.

Copyright © 1968 Doors Music Co.
International Copyright Secured Made In U.S.A. All Rights Reserved

When The Music's Over

Words and Music by
THE DOORS

Copyright © 1967 Doors Music Co.
International Copyright Secured Made In U.S.A. All Rights Reserved

Em
A
D
D♯m
Em
mu-sic's o-ver
turn out the lights,
turn out the lights,
turn out the lights
Bm7
Yeah,
Yeah,
When the
turn out the lights.
For the
A7
E7
mu-sic is your
spe-cial friend.
Dance on fire as

E7
D
D
it in - tends
mu-sic is your
on-ly friend
un -
Em
D
Em
D
D#
til the end,
un - til the
end,
un - til the
Em
(chant style)
Em
A9
end.
Can-cel my sub-scrip-tion to the
Em
A9
Em
D/A
Em
A9
Em
A9
res-ur-rec - tion,
send my cred-en-tials to the
Em
A9
Em
D/A
Em
A9
Em
A7
house of de-ten-tion,
I got some
friends in -

Em7 A7 Em A7 Em A7 Em A9
side. The
Em D/A Em A9 Em D/A
face in the mir-ror won't stop. sfz sfz The girl in the win - dow won't
Em A9 Em D/A Em D
drop. sfz sfz A feast of friends a - live she cried,
Em D/A Em Am Em7 D/A
wait-ing for me___ out - side.
Em A D/A Em Em7 A7 Em A

(Chant - spoken over "Em - A9" chord patterns.)

We're getting tired of waiting around.
Waiting around
with our heads
to the ground.

I hear a very gentle sound.

What have they done to the earth?
What have they done to our fair sister?

Ravaged and plundered
and ripped her and bit her
Stuck her with knives
in the side of the dawn
and tied her with fences
and dragged her down.

I hear a very gentle sound.
With your ear down to the ground—

We want the world and we want it
Now!

Persian night!
See the light!
Save us!
Jesus!
Save us!

Love Her Madly

Words by ROBBIE KRIEGER
Music by THE DOORS

Copyright © 1971 Doors Music Co.
International Copyright Secured Made In U.S.A. All Rights Reserved

Am
Don't you love her mad - ly?
Am7
Want to
F
be her dad - dy?
D
Don't you
Am
love her face?
Am
Don't you love her as she's
E
walk - ing out the door?
Am
Like she did one
Em
thou-sand times be - fore.
Am
Don't you
D7
love her ways?
Tell me

Am
Em
what you say
don't you love her as she's walk-ing out the door?
Am
N.C.
D9
Am7
All your love
all your love
all your love
D7
all your love
all your love is gone,
G
C
So sing a lone - ly song
of a

(Repeat and fade)

Horse Latitudes

When the still sea conspires an armor
And her sullen and aborted
Currents breed tiny monsters,
True sailing is dead.

Awkward instant
And the first animal is jettisoned,
Legs furiously pumping
Their stiff green gallop,
And heads bob up
Poise
Delicate
Pause
Consent
In mute nostril agony
Carefully refined
And sealed over.

Copyright © 1968 Doors Music Co.

The Spy

Words and Music by
JIM MORRISON

Copyright © 1970 Doors Music Co.
International Copyright Secured Made In U.S.A. All Rights Reserved

E7
that you long to hear. I know your
G D E7 A G
deep-est se-cret fear.
1. E N.C.
I'm a spy,
2. D E7 A G E D
I know ev-'ry-thing: Ev-'ry-thing you do;
E D E A G E
Ev-'ry-where you go;
D E
Ev-'ry-one you know.
I'm a spy,
E7 A G E F# G D
I know your deep-est se-cret fear.

E
A
G
E
G
D
I know your deep-est se - cret,
E
E7
I'm a spy
E7
8va
loco
E7
I can see what you do;
E7
And I know.
E7
A

Indian Summer

Words and Music by
JIM MORRISON and
ROBBIE KRIEGER

Copyright © 1970 Doors Music Co.
International Copyright Secured Made In U.S.A. All Rights Reserved

D
1.
2.
rest,
I love
that I
Em7/A
D
meet
in the sum-mer.
Em7/A
D
In - di-an Sum-mer.
D
D
That I

D
I love you
the

D
best,
Bet - ter than

D
all
the

D
rest.